Train Up A Child

by
Chuck Sturgeon

HARRISON HOUSE
Tulsa, Oklahoma

Unless otherwise indicated,
all Scripture quotations are taken from
the *King James Version* of the Bible.

15th Printing
Over 117,000 in Print

Train Up A Child
ISBN 0-89274-120-1
Copyright © 1979 by Chuck Sturgeon
1014 Ramona Drive
Enid, Oklahoma 73703-7113

Published by Harrison House, Inc.
P. O. Box 35035
Tulsa, Oklahoma 74153

Chapter 1
THE NEED AND IMPORTANCE
OF DISCIPLINE

Many homes today are a study in chaos. Tempers flare often as parents yell at their kids and kids yell at their parents. Children rule the home with their incessant whining and threats of rebellion as the parents give-in to avoid another confrontation. Many parents are living a life of fear; dreading what their children will do next, as their children run the gamut of drugs and sex to find out "where it's at." Ultimately, these parents and their children may become the victims of broken homes, ruined reputations, and misdirected lives.

This is not God's plan. When you obey God's commandments, you will have a family that prospers and serves God in harmony.

From God's perspective a family is a *spiritual* union. God has ordained an order of authority in the home. If God is not made the head authority of the home, then the self of every person will assume his own authority. Everyone will do what is right in their own eyes. There will be no order, no consistent standard for each family member to follow. God and His Word need to be Lord over the home. He has given the parents the responsibility of training the children, spirit, soul, and body. *A child needs to have parents who will read and obey God's Word in every area of life —* particularly in child discipline.

Children do not just grow up. There is more to rearing children than giving them a place to stay. Children become what they learn from experiences in the home. Their characters are formed by Mom and Dad. A child's personality strengths and weaknesses, attitudes, and values are formed, in a large part, by his parents.

Children are like plants. If a plant is not watered and nourished properly, given adequate sunlight, and pruned regularly, it will grow, but it will be disfigured. It won't become what God created it to be. Likewise children who

3

lack a balance of parental love, guidance, and discipline will not become the adults God plans for them to be.

God wants us to *DO HIS WORD ALWAYS*, in every area. Deuteronomy 5:29 says, "O that there were such an heart in them, that they would fear me, and keep all my commandments always, that it might be well with them, and with their children for ever." Again He says in Deuteronomy 12:28, "Observe and hear all these words which I command thee, that it may go well with thee, and with thy children after thee for ever, when thou doest that which is good and right in the sight of the Lord thy God."

I have been young, and now am old; yet have I not seen the righteous forsaken, nor his seed begging bread. He is ever merciful, and lendeth; and his seed is blessed (Psalm 37:25-26).

"The fear of the Lord is the beginning of knowledge: but fools despise wisdom and instruction" (Proverbs 1:7). God says fools want to do things their own way. They think they know better than God. "As for God, his way is perfect; the word of the Lord is tried: he is a buckler to all of them that trust in him" (II Samuel 22:31).

Let's see what God says in His Word about child discipline so all may be well with us and our children. "For I know him, that he will command his children and his household after him, and they shall keep the way of the Lord, to do justice and judgment; that the Lord may bring upon Abraham that which He hath spoken of him" (Genesis 18:19).

God spoke blessings upon Abraham. He knew Abraham would receive these blessings as a result of keeping his household in divine order. To God, this included having obedient children. God knew Abraham was a man who would cause his children to grow a certain way. He knew He could trust Abraham to discipline his children.

The word discipline comes from disciple. A disciple is a pupil. Jesus commissioned us to go and TEACH all nations. (Matthew 28:19.) This includes our children. Many Christians have a burning desire to disciple the world for Jesus, but God tells us where to start. "But ye shall receive power, after that the Holy Ghost is come upon you: and ye

4

shall be witnesses unto me both in Jerusalem, and in all Judaea, and in Samaria, and unto the uttermost part of the earth" (Acts 1:8). God instructed the disciples to begin ministering God's Word in Jerusalem where they were, then spread to the rest of the world. We must begin our ministry in our homes *to our own children* before we reach out to the world, or even the next town.

LOVE CHASTENS

The relationship of an earthly father to his children should reflect the relationship of God, our Father, to us, His children.

> *For whom the Lord loveth he chasteneth, and scourgeth every son whom he receiveth. If ye endure chastening, God dealeth with you as with sons; for what son is he whom the father chasteneth not? But if ye be without chastisement, whereof all are partakers, then are ye bastards, and not sons. Furthermore we have had fathers of our flesh which corrected us, and we gave them reverence: shall we not much rather be in subjection unto the Father of spirits, and live? For they verily for a few days chastened us after their own pleasure; but he for our profit that we might be partakers of his holiness. Now no chastening for the present seemeth to be joyous but grievous: nevertheless afterward it yieldeth the peaceable fruit of righteousness unto them which are exercised thereby* (Hebrews 12:6-11).

Now let's apply the above scripture to our family situations. Love chastens. Parents who love their children chasten them. We see that God expects us to be disciplining our children. When we diligently discipline them, our children will yield the peaceable fruits of righteousness in their lives.

Let me add that all people are partakers of chastisement, in one way or another. A person who is seeking God and walking in the light he has will be chastened by a God of love. When he misses it and realizes he has done something contrary to the Word, his spirit grieves and he hastens to

5

repent and please God. Remember, God is a God of love and chastens in love. *HE IS THE FATHER OF SPIRITS AND CHASTENS IN THE SPIRIT.* A person who is walking in satan's territory will be open to the devices of the devil — poverty, sickness, and death. "The thief cometh not, but for to steal, and to kill, and to destroy: I am come that they might have life, and that they might have it more abundantly" (John 10:10).

David said in Psalm 119:67, 71, 75, "Before I was afflicted I went astray: but now have I kept thy word . . . It is good for me that I have been afflicted; that I might learn thy statutes . . . I know, O Lord, that thy judgments are right, and that thou in faithfulness hast afflicted me." Where the King James uses *afflicted* a more accurate word such as *chastened* or *disciplined* should be substituted. David is saying in this psalm that he has endured the chastening of the Lord. He admits that through chastening he has learned to value God's precepts above all else. After receiving chastisement, he no longer strayed from God in that area. The chastening was good. REMEMBER: God is the giver of all good gifts, so don't allow the devil to rob you and blame it on "God's chastening." NO! *GOD CHASTENS IN THE SPIRIT AND IN LOVE.*

Many parents feel they lack the power to discipline their children. This is not true. Remember that in Acts 1:8 Jesus promised we would have all power from the Holy Spirit. If the Greater One is dwelling in you, you have all the power and ability you need. Of course, as parents, it is your God-given responsibility to assume the authority in your home.

Some parents feel they aren't wise enough to deal with their children. God will guide you in the training of your children. As you do the Word, ask Him how to handle situations and He will show you. "I will instruct thee and teach thee in the way which thou shalt go: I will guide thee with mine eye. Be ye not as the horse, or as the mule, which have no understanding: whose mouth must be held in with bit and bridle, lest they come near unto thee" (Psalm 32:8-9). He will never leave you nor forsake you. He is able and willing to help you no matter what circumstances arise.

6

DISCIPLINE NOW

"It is good for a man that he bear the yoke (of divine disciplinary dealings) in his youth" (Lamentations 3:27 Amplified Bible). Children that are not disciplined in their youth suffer for it later in life. Most young people in prisons are there because they finally ran into someone with more authority than they. Everyone is going to have to submit to authority sometime in life. The sooner a child learns to submit to authority, the easier it will be for him to live with it.

If you have not been training your child as the Word teaches, confess it as a sin according to I John 1:9. Then make a strong quality decision to train your child as the Word instructs. Determine to minister discipline and love to your child consistently.

CONFESS THE WORD

All mothers talk to their babies. It is well to *speak your faith* over them. Confess to them what the Word says about them. Tell them who they are in Christ Jesus. Call them proper children. As your children grow, continue to maintain your confession. See your children as proper children as Moses' parents did. (Hebrews 11:23.) Don't even imagine them out in the world getting into trouble. In spite of the situations, hold fast to your confession that your children are proper children.

I have a friend whose daughter left home to get involved in the evil the world offers. He told his daughter that she was a proper child and therefore would not enjoy drinking or taking drugs. He maintained his confession in spite of apparent circumstances. Finally his daughter told him she wasn't having fun with drinking or taking drugs. When she asked her father if she could come home, he told her that he had never considered her gone because she was a proper child.

DON'T TEACH — TRAIN

Train up a child in the way he should go and when he is old, he will not depart from it (Proverbs 22:6).

There is a difference between training and teaching. God wants us to *TRAIN* our children. According to Webster, to train means "to mold the character; to instruct by exercise; drill; to make obedient to orders; to prepare for a contest; to point in an exact direction."

Many parents do not know which direction to point their children because they don't know which way to go themselves. Parents who aren't at rest with God can't train their children correctly. They must be able to flow in the wisdom of God. Parents have to know that they are right when they are controlling and directing their children's lives.

Training is not just teaching a child principles and then letting him decide whether to use them or not. Recently, after I ministered on discipline, a young girl broke into tears. "Mom, why do you think that I have done the things that I have done?" she cried. "Because you let me do anything. I've always wanted you to tell me what I could and couldn't do."

Some parents only teach their children. They don't train them. When you hear a parent continually threatening, "I told you I'd spank you if you don't take out the garbage," over and over until he finally raises his voice in anger, you know that parent has taught that child. *He has taught him not to obey until he gets angry and yells.*

Training a child is different. When a child does not do what he should, you warn him once, then if he disobeys, you administer discipline. You train your child to obey you the first time you speak and in a normal tone! God wants you to train your children.

We need to train our children how to best use what we have taught them; how to apply it to life.

THERE'S A DIFFERENCE

Let's look to the Word of God to see the difference between training and teaching children.

So Hannah rose up after they had eaten in Shiloh, and after they had drunk. Now Eli the priest sat upon a seat by a post of the temple of the Lord. And she was in bitterness of soul, and prayed unto the Lord, and wept sore. And she vowed a vow, and said, O Lord of hosts, if thou wilt indeed look on the affliction of thine handmaid, and remember me, and not forget thine handmaid, but will give unto thine hand-

8

maid a man child, then I will give him unto the Lord all the days of his life, and there shall no razor come upon his head (I Samuel 1:9-11).

Hannah was a woman walking upright before God who desired the blessing of children in her life; she wanted to be fruitful for her husband. She had endured all the persecution she could stand from her husband's other wife. So she came grieving to God. As she prayed in the temple, she began to make a vow before the Lord. She didn't do this lightly — she fully intended to carry it out. God knew she would be faithful.

Notice here that Hannah believed for a man-child. It is possible to believe for a son. Samuel means, *heard of God.* Hannah believed for a son before conception.

In vowing her vow to God, Hannah was pronouncing a dedication upon Samuel. You too can speak words of dedication over your unborn child. After having ten ungodly children, I know a woman who prayed a prayer of dedication over her unborn eleventh child. As time passed, this son became the first of the children to become saved and Spirit-filled. Over the years, he has been used of God to minister to his other brothers and sisters. He has seen many of them confess Jesus as Lord. So dedicate your unborn children to serve Jesus as their Lord. If you didn't, then believe your children will be saved because they belong to your household. (See Acts 16:31.)

And when she had weaned him she took him up with her, with three bullocks, and one ephah of flour, and a bottle of wine, and brought him unto the house of the Lord in Shiloh: and the child was young . . . For this child I prayed; and the Lord hath given me my petition which I asked of him: Therefore also I have lent him to the Lord; as long as he liveth he shall be lent to the Lord. And he worshipped the Lord there (I Samuel 1:24, 27-28).

Hannah granted Samuel to the temple with the condition that he would serve God all his life, and she trained him to go in that way. Samuel served faithfully even as Hannah had trained him. As a child, he ever hastened to do Eli's bidding,

9

even in the middle of the night. As time passed, Samuel became God's man in Israel.

Now let's look at Eli's sons.

> Now the sons of Eli were sons of Belial; they knew not the Lord . . . Now Eli was very old, and heard all that his sons did unto all Israel; and how they lay with the women that assembled at the door of the tabernacle of the congregation. And he said unto them, Why do ye such things? For I hear of your evil dealings by all this people. Nay, my sons; for it is no good report that I hear: ye make the Lord's people to transgress. If one man sin against another, the judge shall judge him: but if a man sin against the Lord, who shall intreat for him? Notwithstanding they hearkened not unto the voice of their father, because the Lord would slay them (I Samuel 2:12, 22-25).

These sons were disobedient and immoral. Notice that Eli used nothing but *WORDS* on his sons. Eli neglected to train his sons and consequently they neglected to listen to him. SCOLDING IS NOT TRAINING. Eli did not train his sons to obey him or the Word. Actually we need to train our children to obey the Word over us as we can miss it sometimes; the Word never does.

THE RESPONSIBILITY IS YOURS

These sons were young men, not little children. God expected Eli to control his grown sons. You are responsible for your children as long as they live with you.

Wherefore kick ye at my sacrifices and at mine offering, which I have commanded in my habitation; and honourest thy sons above me, to make yourselves fat with the chiefest of all the offerings of Israel my people (I Samuel 2:29).

Eli's sons were taking more than their proper share of the priests' privileges. And because Eli allowed them to take unfair advantage of their priestly office, God said Eli was favoring or honoring his sons over Him. *WHEN YOU ALLOW YOUR CHILDREN TO DISOBEY YOU, YOU ARE HONORING THEM BEFORE GOD AND HIS WORD.*

If a child is a disobedient child, then the parent is probably a disobedient parent. God expects you to train your child. If you neglect to do God's Word in this area, you are out of the will of God. Remember too, that spiritual principles will work negatively as well as positively for you. If you sow poor child discipline, you will reap disobedient children as Eli did.

Both Hannah and Eli spent their lives serving God. But while Hannah was obedient to God in training her children (She had five more after Samuel), Eli disobeyed God by not controlling his sons. And Eli's ministry became increasingly less effective as he continued to miss God concerning his sons. The Word says that there was no open vision in Israel under Eli's ministry. (See I Samuel 3:1.)

Finally God completely cut Eli's family out of the priesthood. "For I have told him that I will judge his house for ever for the iniquity which he knoweth; because his sons made themselves vile, and he restrained them not" (I Samuel 3:13).

When they had gotten so far into satan's territory and away from God's protection, the sons and Eli were killed. Not only that, but all Israel was affected by this family's disobedience because the sons lost the Ark of the Covenant to the enemy before their deaths.

From Eli and his sons we can see that not training your children can have disastrous results for you, the children, and the body of Christ.

OBEDIENT FOR GENERATIONS

Besides Samuel, the Word gives us other examples of the benefits resulting from obedient children.

The command which Jonadab the son of Rechab gave to his sons not to drink wine, has been carried out and established (as a custom for more than two hundred years); to this day they drink no wine, but have obeyed their father's command. But I, even I, have persistently spoken to you, but you have not listened and obeyed Me. And Jeremiah said to the house of the Rechabites,

11

Thus says the Lord of hosts, the God of Israel because you have obeyed the commandment of Jonadab your father, and kept all his precepts, and done according to all that he commanded you; Therefore thus says the Lord of hosts, the God of Israel; Jonadab the son of Rechab shall never lack a man (descendant) to stand before Me (Jeremiah 35:14, 18-19 Amplified Bible).

Two hundred years before Jeremiah's ministry, Jonadab had given his sons a command to drink no wine. For two centuries his descendants obeyed Jonadab's words. This obedience to parental authority so pleased God that he promised to give Jonadab male descendants forever.

LET'S CONTINUE

Now that we have seen the importance of having effective discipline in our home the questions that arise next are, "How do I train my children?" and "What does God's Word say about training children?"

There are two elements for effecting training. These are *LOVE* and *CONTROL*. You need 100% of both in dealing with each of your children. You cannot control a child that you do not love, and you cannot love a child that you do not control.

Chapter 2
LOVE

For Christians, the love-walk is of primary importance because we are children of a love God. The Word tells us that God is love. (I John 4:8.) We must extend the same agape-love that we have toward our brethren to our children. In fact, our love-walk must *BEGIN* in the home.

Be ye therefore followers of God, as dear children: And walk in love, as Christ also hath loved us, and hath given himself for us an offering and a sacrifice to God for a sweet-smelling savour (Ephesians 5:1-2).

Love ministers to another person's need without thought of personal gain. God has placed you as head of your home not only to discipline, but also to minister love to your children. God ministers His love to us through His Word. So you should spend time in the Word with your children. Teach them spiritual truths. Teach them their. rights as sons of God, and their authority in Christ Jesus. Let them know that they aren't fighting flesh and blood, but principalities and powers. (See Ephesians 6:12.)

Develop a relationship of mutual trust with your children so you can say about them what God said about Abraham, "For I know him . . ." Let them know you trust them. Give them reason to trust you. Your children should be assured that you are walking close to God so they will be free to seek your counsel. Be on such a level with your children that you can admit your mistakes and ask their forgiveness. As the leader, you must establish this type of relationship. The children will so easily accept a state of mutual trust and respect that you'll find them voluntarily coming to you to seek your forgiveness about minor transgressions that don't even merit discipline.

Fathers, leave your job at the job. The time you spend with your children should be spent in things of mutual interest. Treat your children as little people, not inferior beings. Don't talk down to them. Look into their eyes and have them look straight into your eyes when you are con-

13

versing. This is especially important when you are disciplining them, but practice it always. A child's self-image is not improved by a father or mother who talks to him behind a newspaper.

Show your children that you love them. Don't wait for a special occasion to show affection. Don't hug them only after discipline or only after they've done something especially to please you. Instead, take opportunities to hug and kiss your children just because you love them. Otherwise, you teach them that they must earn your love by performing a certain way.

Most people who have trouble believing that God loves them have had unloving earthly fathers. This is why it is so extremely important for a father to be quick to give his children physical assurances of his love. There is nothing unmanly about a father hugging and kissing his sons.

Always be in an attitude of love with them. Continually try to find things to compliment them about. Many children are disappointing to their parents because their parents have continually emphasized the child's weak points. Don't always be pointing out your child's faults to him. Point out good traits and tell him you have faith in him to do better in his weaker points. *REMEMBER THAT YOUR WORDS HAVE POWER.* Your children will become what you say about them. And they have a way of fulfilling your expectations of them!

My eldest son took to bike riding with ease, but my second son did not. Brian had problems from the start; mainly because I expected him to be clumsy and fail. He never could ride well until after I made Jesus Lord of my life and began to confess positively about him. One day the school was having a bike contest and it seemed that Brian was the worst bicyclist in the crowd. But I told him to "Go win in the name of Jesus." Brian went, knowing his dad believed in him. He came home with the first place honors. Praise the Lord!

It is largely the parents who form their child's character. Before we were saved, my wife and I raised our first son,

14

Mike, very strictly. We demanded top performance of him. When Brian came along, we expected him to do the same things our first boy was doing, although Mike was several years older. I would tell Brian to do something, and when he fumbled around unsuccessfully, I would say irritably, "Sit down Brian; you can't do it right anyway. Mike, you do it." By the time we were saved, Brian had developed a very poor self-image because of our *words* and *attitudes* towards him. Of course, God has since taught us differently, and Brian is developing into a more self-confident person.

BE AN EXAMPLE

Take time with your children. When you want them to do something that is new to them, show them exactly how to perform the task. Don't have an older brother or sister show them. Let each child know that he is equally important to you and worth your time. *REMEMBER, ONE OF THE DEFINITIONS OF TRAIN IS TO INSTRUCT BY EXERCISE.*

Don't have a child do something you won't do yourself. Don't spank a child for being messy if you are messy, or for not making his bed if yours is unmade. Too often the faults of a child reflect those of the parent. If you're having problems with a child lying, check yourself out. He has probably heard you giving out "white" lies as excuses for not going out or for avoiding commitments. In God's eyes, lies are lies; and He doesn't approve of them at all. "That this is a rebellious people, lying children, children that will not hear the law of the Lord" (Isaiah 30:9). And if you're guilty of speaking them, don't whip your child when the school complains that your son lies. Clean up your own act first then be an example to him. If you see your child stealing, hating, ridiculing, etc., check yourself out before you lambast him. You may have to confess the fault and ask him to forgive you for being a poor example.

BE A STIMULATOR, not a reactor. Stop reacting to your child's faults. Look for opportunities to build good traits in your child. Sometimes a child may have a positive trait that the devil will tempt him to misuse in a negative way. A child might be *noisy* (negative) but you can show him that he is a very *ALERT* (positive) child. He could fall into a *"pity party"* (negative) which is *COMPASSION* (positive) misused. A child that is *aggressively over-confident* (negative) needs to be shown the way to cash in on just *CONFIDENCE* (positive). This could go into a long list; but in all these things, it takes the Word and the Holy Spirit to show you, the parent, how to minister the Word positively to your child.

BE AN INITIATOR. Follow your spirit. Stay open to hear from God in dealing with your children. He has the solution for every problem. One lady had a son who was getting to the girl-noticing age. She sought God for wisdom in dealing with him. The Lord told her to get the boy a cat. It seemed strange to her, so the Lord ministered to her that her son needed an outlet to express love. God wanted him to love and pet the cat, instead of the girls. Because she stayed open to God's voice, she found an effective way to meet her son's need before a problem developed. By the way, don't all you parents go out and buy cats; this is just the way the Lord ministered to this lady.

Chapter 3
CONTROL

You cannot *train* a child if you can't *control* him. In many homes, you find two-year-olds running the entire household. If the two-year-old doesn't want to go where the family planned, the whole family stays home. If the two-year-old steals toys from the neighbors, the parents lie to cover up for their little terror. When the two-year-old is caught hitting other kids with a piece of pipe, the parents accuse the other kids of provoking their sweet little baby. There is an element of control in this family. *Everyone is controlled by the two-year-old!* These things ought not to be.

Training your child will often have to be a forceful situation. God has ordained an instrument particularly for you to use to administer control to your child. And He has provided a strategic and well-padded area on your child's body to receive this instrument. Of course, the divine instrument of love is the ROD!

He that spareth his rod hateth his son: but he that loveth him chasteneth him betimes (Proverbs 13:24).

If you want to obey God you have no choice. You must use the rod if you love your child. If you can't make yourself apply the rod, you might as well tell your kids that you hate them. That's what God says. And notice that He says, "Chasten him betimes." This means often — as often as he needs it.

Remember Eli's continual scolding. Don't try to beat your child with words. BROWBEATING WILL NEVER REPLACE BOTTOM BEATING. Browbeating will only cause mental abuse. Children neither respect nor respond positively to mental abuse. But because faith comes by hearing, your negative words will plant faith that he is a failure in his heart. Many parents use other methods in disciplining their kids. In this era, you hear different psychiatrists spouting all kinds of theories. But God's Word is much better than any psychology. And God's Word says a child should be spanked, not Spocked!

APPLY THE ROD

The rod and reproof give wisdom: but a child left to himself bringeth his mother to shame (Proverbs 29:15).

Often when we are out on the road at night, I'll have to tell my boys that they'll receive a spanking when we arrive home, and I may have forgotten. Because they know this is God's will, they will remind me and we'll take care of it. They want to live free of condemnation. They realize the time of correction will be a time of *FORGIVENESS* and *FREEDOM*. Spanking will clear the child's conscience of guilt when the enemy comes to condemn him. He'll be able to look back to the time of correction and know he has been forgiven for the offense and is free of condemnation.

Teach your children to regard the paddle as an instrument of love, not punishment. In fact, use a positive vocabulary with your children. Don't talk about punishment, but about training.

NEVER USE YOUR HAND TO SPANK YOUR CHILD. Instead, employ a paddle that your child will learn to associate with training. *NEVER BRUISE OR BREAK A CHILD'S SKIN.* Never hit a child on the head. Your hands are used to hug or pat affectionately. God never uses His hand to hit us, but to welcome us lovingly into His presence. What a surprise we would have if we went expecting Him to hug us and He slapped us instead. If you discipline with your hands, your child won't know whether you're going to love him or hit him. Haven't you seen children who wince or duck when their father raises his hand?

Spanking is done *FOR* a child, not *TO* him. It is done for the child's good, not because the parent is fed up with his behavior. When you spank a child, it will hurt him, so he will want to avoid similar pain in the future. The next time he is tempted to break that rule, he will remember the spanking. If the punishment is administered consistently, he will associate the pain with the offense. However, improperly administered discipline will result in an oppressed spirit.

Chasten thy son while there is hope, and let not thy soul spare for his crying (Proverbs 19:18).

Don't spare the rod simply because you don't want to hear your child cry. When a child cries, he has submitted himself to receive God-ordained training. God wants us to be tender and teachable, not hard-hearted and rebellious.

Withhold not correction from the child: for if thou beatest him with the rod, he shall not die. Thou shalt beat him with the rod, and shalt deliver his soul from hell (Proverbs 23:13,14).

SPANKING MINISTERS TO THE WHOLE MAN, not just to the body. You are a spirit; you have a soul (mind, will, emotions); and you live in a body. Your child is a spirit. In training him, you should minister to the spirit. Remember that the spirit is ageless, so you can minister in depth.

Getting the Word into the spirit is of primary importance. Then the spirit will reveal spiritual truth to the mind. This is why church nurseries do more harm than good if there is no teaching of the Word. We had our students — kindergarten through 12th grade — listen to guest speakers who came to speak to our adult school. Our kids would sit for over an hour and receive the Word. Visiting ministers were always impressed with their attentiveness. We had trained those children to take notes on what they understood. It continually amazed us to read their summaries of the sermons. They were catching hold of the truths in God's Word.

When you train a child, you encourage him to submit his selfish will. A person with a selfish will won't make Jesus his Lord. A person who knows how to submit to the authority of parents will not find it difficult to accept Jesus as Lord. The child, who knows his parents love him and has been trained to obey their authority, will find it easy to allow a loving God to control his life.

The rod should be used to correct *WRONG THOUGHTS, WORDS,* and *DEEDS.* When a child commits a trespass in the physical realm, we usually are quick to deal with it. But how many parents allow their children to speak words of disrespect about them or other authority: "My old man"; "That dumb teacher"; "The rules of this school are stupid."

The thought realm of a child is the responsibility of his parents, too. *THOUGHTS ARE POWERFUL.* They determine a person's actions. Teach your children to think on good things.

19

Finally, brethren, whatsoever things are true, whatsoever things are honest, whatsoever things are lovely, whatsoever things are of good report; if there be any virtue, and if there by any praise, think on these things (Philippians 4:8).

Sometimes I know by the spirit what my son is thinking. Right then I'll take him to the bedroom. I'll tell him that God has shown me that he was thinking wrong thoughts. I'll have him tell me what he was thinking. Then I talk to him about it and administer the rod, if necessary. When a child realizes he can't even get away with thinking bad thoughts, he'll learn to cast down imaginations and take every thought captive to the obedience of the Word. (See II Corinthians 10:5.)

Foolishness is bound in the heart of a child; but the rod of correction shall drive it far from him (Proverbs 22:15).

BENEFITS

Not only will your child be *WISE* as a result of discipline, but he and you will benefit in other ways too.

Children, obey your parents in the Lord: for this is right. Honour thy father and mother; which is the first commandment with promise; That it may be well with thee, and thou mayest live long on the earth (Ephesians 6:1-3).

An obedient child will have a *LONG LIFE*. Disobedience to parental authority is one reason why life spans got shorter in the Old Testament. God promises His protection on a person who learns to obey his parents. Any parent that loves his child desires God's protective power in the child's life. This is a sure way to have it!

When you discipline your child according to God's Word, the child will begin to *DISCIPLINE HIMSELF*. A self-disciplined person is a successful person in every area. It takes self-discipline to get up in the morning, to hold a steady job, to serve God diligently. The sooner a child learns to control himself, the more capable he will be in dealing with the responsibilities in life.

A home containing well-disciplined children is a restful situation. "Correct thy son, and he shall give thee rest; yea, he shall give delight unto thy soul" (Proverbs 29:17). Most people today are not delighted or at rest about their children. In fact, the average parents are worried to distraction about their kids. They are actually in fear about what Junior may do next to shame them. It is not a restful situation. But if your son is well-disciplined, you know he will bring you no shame. You know he is doing only good things and earning a good reputation.

It is an honor to have an obedient child. People will love to come to your home because of the peace and rest in it. You will not have to point out your children's good behavior. If they have been trained according to the Word of God, people will notice the difference. "Even a child is known by his doings, whether his work be pure, and whether it be right" (Proverbs 20:11). Thus you can delight in him and be at rest.

DO'S AND DON'TS

And ye fathers, provoke not your children to wrath: but bring them up in the nurture and admonition of the Lord (Ephesians 6:4).

Children, obey your parents in all things: for this is well pleasing unto the Lord. Fathers, provoke not your children to anger, lest they be discouraged (Colossians 3:20-21).

How does a parent provoke a child?

One of the most flagrant ways is to be *INCONSISTENT*. Many parents discipline according to their moods. On their good days a child can commit an atrocity and not be disciplined at all. On bad days the same kid gets spanked for sneezing too loudly. Of course this discourages a child. He doesn't know any definite bounds and will eventually rebel out of pure frustration. It takes diligence, single-mindedness, and singleness of purpose to discipline a child properly. It's not an easy thing to do. A selfish love wants an easier way, but a person motivated by the love of God is willing to maintain the level of consistency that the Word demands.

Another thing that will provoke a child is to *DISCIPLINE* him *IN ANGER*. When you get *ANGRY*, you are more wrong than

21

the child and any discipline you administer will only drive the child farther from you. Wait, if you must, until you control yourself so you can discipline in love.

There was a young boy in our school who always seemed to rub me the wrong way. He seemed to spend his time devising trouble. One day I got mad and jerked him angrily out of devotions. The whole school knew that Mr. Sturgeon was fed up with that boy. The first thing I had to do when we got to my office was ask him to forgive me for losing my temper. That surprised him. Then we got down to the Word. After taking time to review these scriptures on discipline, he said he needed a spanking. That boy grew in faith and obedience that year. At the year-end banquet, his father proudly testified that when he told his son to do a task, he knew it would be done; he wouldn't even have to check to see.

When you have more than one child, *TREAT THEM EQUALLY* in giving and in disciplining. When you are more lenient with one than with another, you will discourage the one you are harder on. If you do let one child have a privilege that you forbid to the others, let the other children know it is because that one has shown he can act responsibly in that area. Be sure they all understand that Bob has behaved maturely enough to take out the car, not that you love him more. When you treat your children equally, they will become equally responsible and well-disciplined. Families with obedient and disobedient children have treated their children differently.

Modern psychology sometimes dictates treating children differently according to their personalities, but God has only one type of discipline for every child.

My son, despise not the chastening of the Lord; neither be weary of his correction: For whom the Lord loveth he correcteth; even as a father the son in whom he delighteth (Proverbs 3:11-12).

My son attend unto my wisdom, and bow thine ear to my understanding . . . Lest thou give thine honour unto others, and thy years unto the cruel . . . And say, How have I hated instruction, and my heart despised reproof (Proverbs 5:1, 9, 12).

DON'T ALLOW YOUR CHILDREN TO DESPISE CHASTENING. You must be positive and reinforce the idea that chastening is an element of loving. Teach them to respect the authority that God has placed over them in the home, school, community, and nation. Discipline them for disrespectful attitudes, as well as disobedience.

DON'T ALLOW YOUR CHILDREN TO REBEL. "For rebellion is as the sin of witchcraft, and stubbornness is as iniquity and idolatry" (I Samuel 15:23).

Remember that you are the standard that your children will look to in dealing with life. If you want them to have respect for outside authority, you too must show respect.

Let every soul be subject unto the higher powers. For there is no power but of God: the powers that be are ordained of God. Whosoever therefore resisteth the power, resisteth the ordinance of God: and they that resist shall receive to themselves damnation (Romans 13:1-2).

If the law says drive 55 mph, be certain that your kids will notice if you are doing 65 mph. And if Daddy can break the law, then it must be okay for everyone to. If Dad brings home little things from the factory, Junior may begin bringing home little things he picked up in the store or at the neighbors. If Mom dents the car and disclaims any knowledge of it, Suzy will see that it is all right to lie, as long as you don't get caught. Parents should be honorable to be worthy of receiving their children's respect and honor.

DON'T ALLOW YOUR CHILDREN TO COMPLAIN. "And when the people complained, it displeased the Lord" (Numbers 11:1).

DON'T ALLOW YOUR CHILDREN TO BE BITTER. "Looking diligently lest any man fail of the grace of God; lest any root of bitterness springing up trouble you, and thereby many be defiled" (Hebrews 12:15).

Even if a child is wrongfully condemned by someone, a root of bitterness shouldn't be allowed to rise in his heart against that person. Teach your child to walk in forgiveness toward everyone. If your child wants to complain about a person or a situation, instruct him to speak his *faith* about it instead. *Have him call things that are not as though they were.* If the situation or person is wrong, God will move on your child's behalf.

DON'T ALLOW YOUR CHILD TO BE SLOTHFUL OR WASTEFUL. Teach him to be a good steward of his time, money, and possessions. "He also that is slothful in his work is brother to him that is a great waster" (Proverbs 18:9). Waster in the Hebrew means destroyer. Satan is the destroyer. The less responsible with time and money a person is, the more he opens himself to satan's ravages and shuts himself off from God's blessings.

DON'T MAKE YOUR CHILD DO SOMETHING YOU WON'T DO YOURSELF. Always be sure your instructions are in line with the Word. Ephesians says to obey your parents "in the Lord." If you get out of the Word, have your child trained well enough to recognize it. And when he sets you straight, ask him to forgive you.

DON'T RIDICULE, BELITTLE, SCORN, OR EMBARRASS YOUR CHILD. Love is supposed to *edify* and *encourage* a person to achieve his fullest potential, not tear down. Avoid spanking him in public, especially in front of his peers. Always have a compliment for your child, especially after discipline. Even if you can't find much positive, mention something.

At the first of the school year, we had school in a hotel. One little boy threw hard-boiled eggs out the window and poured water on the people sitting a floor below in the lobby. Of course, this kind of behavior didn't do much for school-hotel relations! When I finished spanking this boy, it was a real challenge to find something to compliment him on. Finally I told him that he certainly wore his uniform neatly. He walked away chastened, but built up because he wore his clothes well. Once he knew he could please us, he began to try to do well overall. We didn't have much more trouble with that boy. When the first quarter ended, he had the highest average in the school.

Sometimes we over plan a child's life. Parents need to operate in the wisdom of God to know when to make the decisions and when to let their child work a problem out himself. Our job is to train the child in the way he should be and then let him go that way on his own.

Once you teach your child what the Word says about an area of his life, train him to *DO* the Word. Once he learns the truths in Luke 6:38 and Malachi 3:10, train him to tithe, give, and believe for a return.

My oldest son Mike has always been diligent to tithe and give of his money. One summer he wanted extra money so he decided to mow lawns. The only problem was he didn't have access to a lawn mower. One day a man down the street, who had never been to our house, came to see Mike. He owned quite a bit of rental property around town. He said he wanted Mike to mow all his lawns. He also said he would supply the mower, the gas, and transportation about town and to the dump to dispose of the grass. God provided.

My sons have learned to apply their faith in other areas, too. They have believed God for a horse, a bicycle, a mini-bike, and even a round-trip airplane flight. Teach your children that Jesus gives all good gifts and that *THEIR FAITH* will work for them.

Many parents don't like all the rules God wants them to enforce. "But I want my child to be free," they declare.

And I will walk at liberty: for I seek thy precepts (Psalms 119:45).

Real freedom is gained when children have learned to receive God's direct guidance. Some people are in bondage to freedom. They flitter around being free, but *neglect to DO the Word.* And they usually end up confused with their lives in a mess.

Chapter 4
INSTITUTING DIVINE DISCIPLINE

Now that you've studied the why and how of divine discipline, you're wondering how to institute it into *your* household. If you realize that you've missed God in dealing with your children, don't despair. Your household may be a mess, but God promises He can fix even the biggest fiasco.

Come, and let us return unto the Lord . . . and he will bind us up (Hosea 6:1).

As you ask Him to forgive you for mishandling your children, believe Him to heal your family. He will.

And I will restore to you the years that the locust hath eaten, the cankerworm, and the caterpiller, and the palmerworm . . . (Joel 2:25).

Parents should read and study the scriptures presented, aloud together, and make a strong quality decision to apply them to their family. Parents must be in total agreement in this or they won't achieve the consistency that their children need. Even if you can't agree with everything in this book, you must agree with each other and the Word.

When you are certain you stand solidly together on every point, then vow a vow together before God that you will do His Word in training your children. Don't make this vow if you don't intend to keep it or if you only want to try it for a while. (See Deuteronomy 23:21-23.) Be sure to speak the vow out loud, as *YOUR WORDS HAVE CREATIVE POWER.*

For verily I say unto you, That whosoever shall say unto this mountain, Be thou removed, and be thou cast into the sea; and shall not doubt in his heart, but shall believe that those things which he saith shall come to pass; he shall have whatsoever he saith (Mark 11:23).

After you have told God that you're serious, arrange a meeting with your children. Make it a special, uninterrupted session. Turn off the television and take the phone off the hook. Go through these scriptures thoroughly with them, explaining what they mean and how they apply to them. Make sure they understand that this is God's perfect way and that you as a family desire to please Him in this. Give them a chance to ask questions.

Lay down the basics, firmly. You might say something like this. "Kids, from now on when you do something wrong, we're not going to yell and scream at you. We will just tell you in a normal tone to empty the trash. If you don't empty the trash, then we will give you swats for it. We will always do it in your bedroom and here is the instrument that we'll do it with. It's just that simple. You are obedient children and you are going to submit yourselves totally to this."

In laying down the rules, do it in love. Don't act like a general in the Army. Remember that God's way is love's way. Don't start out with so many rules that you stifle them or put them in fear.

Don't expect too much of a child. A 6-year-old can't perform at the level of a 10-year-old. Besides, your neglect of doing the Word has caused them to be what they are now anyway. *BE REASONABLE.*

Parents, *WRITE DOWN YOUR RULES* so you all have a clear idea what they are. Don't make any rules you won't enforce. Start small.

Also, don't spank them for any previous offenses. Some parents want to catch-up for their past leniency. This is not the way to begin. Start fresh with the night of the meeting, after the kids have an understanding of how things stand.

Now that you have made discipline by the Word clear to your children, you must enforce it consistently. The first few days you may find yourself using the rod frequently. After a few days of this, your children will begin to see that you mean business and the number of spankings will decrease markedly.

THE PROPER PROCEDURE

Remember that training involves love as well as control. The time when you take a disobedient child back to the particular room you have designated as the room for discipline must be a time of love and control.

Let's take a closer look at what goes on in this room.

Make sure your child understands what wrong he has committed, and can tell you why he is receiving discipline at this time. Have him tell you the nature of his offense.

Train your child to submit to the spanking willingly. Have him bend over with his hands placed on something in front of him like the back of a chair or the bed. Tell him to keep his hands away from his "seat." If he puts his hands on his seat, keep spanking. You can pray for his hands later, and he will learn to submit to the spanking.

Many children try to run from their parents. My youngest son tried. I told him, "I can outrun you. Even if in the natural I could not outrun you, God will give me His power as He did Elijah, and I'll catch up with you anyway. I will continue to spank you as you run. Daddy will not quit until you willingly submit to it in the bedroom. You have a free will and can choose a quick private spanking in the bedroom or a long embarrassing one all over the neighborhood in front of all your friends." You will have to chase your child only once if you do this.

After you have used the rod and your child has totally submitted to it, pray with him. Have him ask God to forgive him. Then you pray. Confess the Word that is working in his life. And then love him. Hug him and tell him you love him and forgive him. Find some positive things to tell him about himself.

Be consistent. Everytime your child doesn't obey you the *FIRST TIME* you tell him to do something, discipline him. If he disobeys in the same area more than once, treat the offense as though it were the first time it happened. Don't bring up past mistakes to a child's memory. He has been forgiven of his past transgressions by you and God. You know God forgets your offenses when you ask Him for forgiveness. Treat your child with the same grace.

After you spank your child, do not inflict punishment. *God's not in the business of taking things away from people.* Don't ground him or take his bike away from him for a week. He ordained the rod as the mode of discipline, and He considers the rod adequate to do the job.

Chapter 5
CHRISTIAN SCHOOLS

Have you ever stopped to think about how much opportunity your child's school has to influence him? Do you realize the school has your child more waking hours than you do for nine months every year, from the time he is five until he leaves home? It's good for you, the parents, to be involved in the school. If you're involved in it, you'll have an idea of what is going on there. And you will have a say-so in what they teach your child.

Public schools today generally reflect the world and its values. And this is what they are transmitting to your children.

Because the schools have such a tremendous influence on your child, you should continually lift the school, its policies, and staff up in intercession before God. Believe God to put His people on the staff and expect Him to do it.

Thank God that there is an even better solution!

In these last days God is raising up Christian educators who have a desire to minister full-time to children. So, they are founding Christian schools. Can you imagine the impact children will make on the world, who are raised in a Christian home and taught Christian precepts daily in a Christian school? Can you imagine children who are *taught never to doubt God's Word?*

In the fall of 1976, we began a Christian School, Bread of Life, for Kindergarten-12th grades. "And all thy children shall be taught of the Lord; and great shall be the peace of thy children" (Isaiah 54:13). The results of the first year's operation convinced me that no Christian child should be forced into a public school situation, if at all possible.

Too often we send vulnerable children off into a breeding ground of all the world vices, expecting them to single-handedly clean up their environment. We look to the children to stand firmly against the persecution of their classmates and lead all the mockers to Christ.

We are sending our kids out to do what most adults won't do.

How much better to send your child to a Christian school where he has the freedom to develop his faith so that when he is older and has a more thorough understanding of the Word, he can be a successful witness for Christ, rather than a humiliated, embarrassed, futile Christian martyr at the age of ten.

And don't worry about the other kids in public school. The Holy Spirit has a way of bringing the truth to hungry children. While my boys no longer attend public school, they have had many opportunities to witness to their neighbors and lead several of them to Jesus.

By sending your children to a Christian school, you are not isolating them from the world. Instead, you are *EQUIP-PING THEM* with the power and ability to be successful Christian people in the world.

Most of the youth ministers will admit that Sunday School and youth group meetings are not sufficient to turn a child into God's servant, anymore than one or two meals a week will develop a strong body. *EVERYONE NEEDS A STEADY DIET OF GOD'S WORD TO GROW SPIRIT-UALLY*. A good Christian school will provide it.

What an opportunity to direct a child in the way he should go. We began the year with a varied group of children. Some had parents in the ministry, some were from broken homes. Some were saved and Spirit-filled, others were actually antagonistic toward spiritual teachings. Some had been praying for a Christian school, others were there because public school had kicked them out. We treated them all the same with large doses of the Word, lots of love, and strong applications of the paddle, as needed. And we watched God change lives and mold children into imitators of Christ Jesus.

Our students learned the power of prayer as we would gather together to agree in the name of Jesus that some particular need would be met. They believed God successfully for material blessings for themselves and for others. They saw God heal their own bodies, their sick friends, and even injured pets.

One day one of the primary boys stayed home sick. The other five and six-year-olds missed him, so they prayed for his healing. An hour later, a happy, healed boy appeared at the classroom door.

Children are eager to do the Word. They only need to be taught how.

We taught not only that God heals, but that the believer can walk in divine health. Our children believed the Word. After the first seven weeks of school, we gave the kids a day off for BEING WELL. They earned it. Not one child had missed a single day of school in seven weeks.

What an opportunity a Christian school has to mold characters, to point children to the Way — Jesus!

Your kids deserve a chance to become established firmly on the Word of God before they have to face the doubt and unbelief of this present world.

To contact Chuck Sturgeon, write:
Chuck Sturgeon
1014 Ramona Dr.
Enid, OK 73703-7113
Feel free to include your prayer requests and comments when you write.

Train Up A Child is available
at your local bookstore.

HARRISON HOUSE
P. O. Box 35035 • Tulsa, OK 74153